What Are You Doing?

The uncomfortable truth about how you ~~spend~~ WASTE time at work

To Causer, Monkey and Loobie.

CONTENTS

CONTENTS

INTRODUCTION

"It is not that we have a short time to live, but that we waste a lot of it."

Seneca

There's a reason you use the phrase 'spending time'. You have a limited supply that you started using the moment you were born. Depending on your age, you might already be halfway through. Now isn't that a sobering thought?

Time is your most precious resource. You can't buy more, and you can't make more. But you can make the most of the time you already have – and this book will show you how to take back control. It's not just about doing more or being more productive. It's about respecting your time and teaching others to respect it too.

Imagine how different your life would be if, from the very beginning of your education, you had been taught how to understand your time, how to manage your time, how to get the most from your time and how to protect your time?

This book is for you if you feel that the only thing standing between you and success in business is having more time. It will help you to reclaim each of the 11 hours the average person currently loses each week, making you 10 weeks richer across an entire year. Ten weeks! Imagine how much more you'll be able to do and how successful you'll be with an extra 10 weeks at your disposal. That's over a fifth of your working time.

Although you might not realise it, most of your time is lost in three areas:

- You go to lots of meetings - many of which you know are a complete waste of time.

- You spend hours each day trawling through your inbox, reading and sending emails. Only a small number are actually relevant to you.

- Each day brings unexpected interruptions - many of which are for trivial reasons. You simply don't need to be interrupted in the first place.

2

Does this surprise you? Perhaps not. You might even be nodding while you read this, thinking to yourself, "Yes, that sounds familiar." But aren't you at least shocked by how accepting you are of the situation?

How many times have you thought, "Yes, I am busy, but I should be, I'm a manager."?

How many times have you emerged from a poorly managed meeting, muttering about having lost another hour from your life that you'll never get back, only to turn up to the very same meeting the following week?

How many times have you taken on or finished someone else's work for them having convinced yourself it's just quicker if you do it yourself?

Perhaps you've completed a leadership development course but can't find time to apply the new tools and techniques you've learnt. After all, you already have little or no time to deal with the work that is already on your plate!

Perhaps you believe you have no choice, or that spending so much time at work comes with the territory of being in business or being successful.

If this sounds like you, don't worry, you're not alone. Millions of people are struggling with exactly the same challenges every minute of every day in organisations across the world.

In the pages that follow you'll be introduced to five simple steps that form the heart of the Diary Detox. These five steps will show you the true value of the activities you fill your diary with every day - and help you to create a diary that contains only valuable, targeted activities that will achieve your goals and give you back time. As a result, you'll notice that you simply don't need to do some activities anymore, either because they're no longer required, or because someone else is better placed to take them on.

This is not going to be easy

A board director, having completed the Diary Detox, summarised it as "simple, but not easy".

She explained that in going through each of the five Diary Detox steps for the first time, she felt scrutinised, even criticised, by her own diary. Her diary told a story about her use of time and it wasn't a story she enjoyed hearing.

You will likely find this a challenging journey. You, too, might not enjoy the story your diary will tell you. While the Diary Detox steps that you will discover are very simple, following them regularly takes discipline and determination.

Just like starting a diet or a new exercise regime, the activities are not complicated, but going to the gym when you're tired, or resisting a snack when you're stressed, is an entirely different story.

If you're not ready to take on the challenge, put this book down for another day. It'll save you some time now, in the short term. However, if you've had enough of being a slave to your diary and you are ready to take back control of your time, read on.

Why Diary Detox works

You get to reflect regularly

Diary Detox is a mirror. A mirror that reflects what you do at work. Just like any other mirror, to see your reflection you need to stand in front of it. If you're honest with yourself as you work through the pages of this book, then you'll see yourself, and what's really going on. Only by regularly and consciously taking a look at yourself and what you do with your time do you get to truly reflect, and reflection is a fundamental element of learning and improvement.

You understand the value of everything you do

A number of popular time-management approaches ask you to do 'The One Thing' that will have the greatest impact, to work on the urgent-important activity before anything else, or to 'Eat That Frog' by dealing with the least desirable thing on your to-do list first.

But, what if that one thing adds no value? What if the urgent-important activity isn't as urgent or important as you first thought? And what if you don't need to eat the frog at all? And how would you know?

Diary Detox provides an objective way to identify the value of everything you do, allowing you to remove unnecessary tasks from your to-do list and to focus only on what will achieve your goals.

You are able to see the value of everything you do

Knowing the value of the activities that fill your diary is one thing but seeing their value is far more powerful. Colour-coding activities in your diary helps that value stand out.

You might already categorise activities in your diary using colour. For example, meetings might be red, travel green, personal time yellow etc. But instead of colour-coding by activity type, what if you could use colours to highlight the difference between activities that are, and are not, worthy of your time?

Diary Detox provides a way of colour-coding the activities in your diary based on activity value rather than activity type. Unproductive meetings look different from productive ones. Productive meetings look different from super-productive ones.

Once you can spot the activities that add little or no value, you start to question why they add no value. You might even start to question why the activities got into your diary in the first place.

"I colour all of my client meetings GOLD!"

A business owner had always used the colour yellow for ALL client meetings because yellow reminded her of gold and gold reminded her of money.

The problem? Not all client meetings were successful at bringing in money. The business owner realised that to know the difference between client meetings that add value and those that don't, she would have to change her approach.

Having made the change, she realised which client meetings were less successful at bringing in money. That realisation caused her to reflect on why they were less successful. She changed how she prepared for each meeting and saw improved results immediately.

You know if you're on track

What are you expected to do at work to be successful, and how will you achieve it? To answer that right now, you might point to your job description or your role profile. These likely outline a set of activities that you need to carry out as part of your day-to-day job. But, are you sure those activities are sufficient? Are you sure those activities are yielding the right results?

Should you instead aim to produce a set of outcomes? And what outcomes should you be expected to deliver? To answer that, you might point to your objectives, agreed, if at all, as part of your annual or semi-annual review. What if those objectives are incomplete or non-specific? What if those objectives change but neither you nor your boss notice? What if you get off-track without realising?

It sounds ridiculous, right? But for many of us what we are supposed to achieve, and our progress, is uncertain. And we might only discover that we've missed our objectives at our next annual review. By then it's too late.

Discovery and review of your objectives is a weekly activity within the Diary Detox. You will learn to take an impartial look at whether your objectives are complete, and whether the activities in your diary will keep you on track to deliver them.

You plan ALL of your time

Most wasted time is lost by accident through lack of planning.

> ### "Why do I waste time reading that?"
>
> One business owner admitted that she spent an hour every morning reading a news digest that she knew added no value whatsoever. She realised that the only reason she chose to read the digest was because her diary was always empty every morning at that specific time. She filled the space with whatever was sitting in front of her in her inbox.

Imagine that you only use your diary for scheduled meetings and nothing else. The rest of your diary would be empty, right? What will you do when you get to that empty space?

Perhaps you'll resume whatever task you were doing before your previous meeting. You might turn to your ever-growing to-do list, but which item do you tackle first? The one at the top, the one that seems easiest, the one that seems hardest, or the one with the earliest due date? With all those choices, you'd be forgiven for closing your eyes, waving your finger, pointing and hoping for the best.

Perhaps you'll turn to your inbox and become distracted by the many emails sitting there that could probably wait or be discarded.

You might allow yourself to be interrupted by what is going on around you, or by whoever throws their problem in your direction.

Unplanned time risks being unfocused, and the less focused your time, the more likely it is to be time that you waste.

Diary Detox will show you how to plan your week so that every moment in your diary is part of a considered decision about what most needs your attention, making it less likely that you'll get side-tracked and waste precious time. Those around you will have to think twice about interrupting you because they will have to make a case for stealing your time. You'll get to weigh the value of any new activity against the value of the activities that you will have planned into your diary in advance.

You get better at dealing with interruptions

It's a fact of life, wherever you work there will always be interruptions. Open-plan offices are known to damage productivity. At the first sight of a challenge, colleagues decide to share their problem with whomever is closest… you!

Even if you work from home with no colleagues around you, your phone, email, family and friends offer myriad opportunities for interruption. You can turn off notifications, only check email at specific times, or put a 'Do Not Disturb' sign up on your office door. Still, interruption is inevitable, and you need a strategy for dealing with interruptions when they occur.

Diary Detox includes a tool, the Spot Diary Detox, that will keep the length of any unavoidable interruption to an absolute minimum.

You remain in full control

You are in full control over how you use your time. You always have been. After all, only you know your life and what you want from it. Diary Detox won't tell you what to do. Instead it will disrupt your natural tendency to use time without fully thinking through the consequences and give you the final say on how you use your time.

How to use this book

The Diary Detox has three mains parts: The Initial Diary Detox, the Weekly Diary Detox and the Spot Diary Detox, each building upon the part that precedes it. It is therefore vital that you work through each part in sequence. There is also one critical tool that you will use throughout the Diary Detox.

The Diary Detox Categories

The Diary Detox Categories are the secret sauce of the Diary Detox. They show you the value of every activity you do and will help you to differentiate between the activities that you need to do and those that you can delegate, do less of, or dispense with altogether.

Part One - The Initial Diary Detox

The Initial Diary Detox is a one-time activity that will introduce you to the five Diary Detox steps: Diary, Evaluate, Target, Opportunity and X-change - DETOX.

By practising those steps on a past week in your diary, you will see how you have been spending your time, how you should have been spending your time, and whether they are one and the same.

The Initial Diary Detox is where your process of reflection begins.

Part Two - The Weekly Diary Detox

The Weekly Diary Detox is the most important habit to get into that will disrupt and improve your relationship with time. It is a weekly activity, lasting up to thirty minutes, that will ensure your diary remains detoxed going forward. As part of those thirty vital minutes, you will use the five Diary Detox steps to reflect on your previous week, and to make sure your diary for the upcoming week contains all the activity you need to meet your targets and add value.

Part Three - The Spot Diary Detox

The Spot Diary Detox is an on-demand tool for dealing with unexpected interruptions. It's particularly useful if you find it hard to say no to colleagues' demands on your time. In a matter of seconds, you'll use the five Diary Detox steps to disrupt your automatic instinct to give your time away. People will not respect your time until you do. The Spot Diary Detox is where gaining respect for your own time starts.

You'll need your diary

You will need access to an electronic diary like Microsoft Outlook, Google Calendar or Apple Calendar, that has the ability to colour-code activities.

If you already use colours to categorise your diary, the Diary Detox will most likely require you to change your current colour scheme and approach. This is because the Diary Detox focuses on colour-coding by value, rather than by activity type.

Keep it real

To get the most from your Diary Detox, you should work through it, with your diary, in real-time, as you read this book. With each chapter, you will be asked to carry out tasks. Do the tasks immediately to get the most out of them.

When there is a task for you to do, you'll see the words:

COME BACK WHEN DONE.

That is your cue to carry out the task and only continue with the rest of the chapter when that task is complete.

Commonly used information

As you progress through your Diary Detox, you will need to capture information in tables that you will refer back to from time to time. While a picture of each table is included in the relevant chapter, you should capture your information in the copies provided on pages 95 and 96. You have the option of cutting-out those pages so that you can keep the tables alongside the book as you work.

For your convenience, a colour copy of each figure in this book can also be found at www.diarydetox.com/resources/book.

Just go with it

Everything you're about to read has been specifically designed to get you to the point where you can use the Weekly Diary Detox and the Spot Diary Detox. As you work through this book, you might wonder how you're going to remember everything. Don't worry, you don't need to. Just go with it and all will become clear.

THE DIARY DETOX
CATEGORIES

"Ordinary people think
merely of spending time, great
people think of using it."

Arthur Schopenhauer

Every activity in your working life can be assigned one of seven categories, each describing the value you get from that activity. Understanding the Diary Detox Categories and how to use them will help you decide if what you do each day is actually worth your time.

To introduce the Diary Detox Categories, relax and watch a story unfold where you'll see each of them in action.

A person walks into a bar...

Imagine you walk into your favourite bar or pub. You approach the bar and standing there are three bartenders. You catch the eye of the one closest to you and order a drink. While you wait, you take a look at the menu and once your drink arrives, you order some food. As you find somewhere to sit, you notice that there is another person working in the bar, collecting glasses and wiping tables.

DOING

Definition: You're producing something or carrying out a task.

The bartender is DOING. She is hands-on and carrying out the main activity of the business. The person collecting glasses and wiping tables is also DOING.

Other examples:

- Creating a document
- Sending an email
- Submitting an expense claim
- Necessary travel

As you enjoy your drink and wait for your food, you glance around and notice the supervisor.

While he helps out with general tasks, he also appears to be looking around, keeping an eye on making sure that everyone is doing their job and that the customers are happy.

MONITORING

Definition: You're checking to see that things are as expected.

The supervisor is MONITORING. He is checking to make sure that everyone is DOING their job.

Other examples:

- Having a 121 meeting to check on progress
- Reading a financial report
- Reviewing a document
- Attending a project review meeting
- Stocktaking

HINT: Anytime you hear the words, checking, reviewing, looking over, keeping an eye on, or catching up, it's likely that MONITORING is in progress.

As the supervisor scans the room, you notice him looking at one particular bartender who is focused entirely on her phone.

Meanwhile, a customer is left waiting.

FLOATING

Definition: You're not adding value or you're not sure what value you're adding.

The bartender is FLOATING. While she should be serving, she is concentrating on her phone.

FLOATING is wasting time. Not knowing what value you are adding is also FLOATING because if you don't know what value you're adding, it's likely that you're not adding any.

Other examples:

- Attending a meeting without understanding why you're there.
- Writing a report that you believe will never be read.
- Travelling to a meeting that could have been held via video or telephone.
- Procrastinating

You watch the supervisor walk over to the bartender and ask that they put their phone away and serve the waiting customer.

DIRECTING

Definition: You're giving instruction or assigning tasks.

The supervisor is DIRECTING. He sees that the customer is having to wait for the bartender and chooses to intervene by telling the bartender to put their phone away and get back to work.

The key phrase is 'instructing'. DIRECTING is all about telling someone what needs to be done, giving exact instructions.

Other examples:

- Demonstrating how something should be done.
- Giving an order
- Giving permission

As your food is delivered (DOING), you notice the owner of the bar sitting at another table surrounded by paperwork and watching everything that's going on in the bar (MONITORING). She watches as the supervisor spots and corrects the bartender's error. This is exactly what the owner expected so there's no need for her to get involved. However, she has a puzzled look on her face.

There are no more customers at the bar. The bartenders have served everyone and have each turned their attention to their phone. All the while, the person collecting the glasses and wiping tables is still busy.

There's nothing particularly wrong with this situation. After all, the bartenders' job is to work behind the bar and the glass collector's job is to collect glasses. But it doesn't look and feel right to the owner. The owner appears to have had an idea.

THINKING

Definition: You are taking time to think about vision, strategy, a plan or obstacles to achieving them.

The owner is THINKING, looking at the overall situation rather than at individual employees or tasks. She is considering how the overall operation of the bar could be improved, to work more efficiently, to be a better place to work or a better place for people to visit.

THINKING is the most undervalued and underperformed activity in business, often due to an overabundance of DOING, MONITORING, DIRECTING and FLOATING. A lack of THINKING prevents seeing the bigger picture and can result in missing out on improvements.

Other examples:

- Considering vision or strategy
- Brainstorming with colleagues
- Being coached or mentored
- Going for a walk or taking exercise to ponder

The bar owner calls the supervisor over. You hear the owner explain that she has noticed the bartenders 'switch off' when there are no customers at the bar. All the while, the glass collector is still running around because there is always something to do (cleaning tables, sweeping the floor etc.).

The owner suggests that the glass collector becomes part of one team and that responsibility for collecting glasses and wiping tables is shared by all the bartenders. That way, when there are no customers at the bar, there is always something to do and no one runs out of work.

The supervisor likes the idea and mentions that they have also noticed that from time to time there is a rush of customers and the bartenders are swamped for a short period. The supervisor suggests that glass collecting could take a temporary back seat when there are lots of customers and that the priority could switch to serving.

The owner likes this extra angle and is now even more keen on the idea. They both agree that the plan they've discussed could work. The owner asks when the best opportunity would be to make the change.

The supervisor suggests a conversation with the bartenders and the glass collector first, to share the idea. Once everyone is on board with the idea, the glass collector will be trained by shadowing the bartenders for some shifts. The supervisor and owner agree to temporarily cover the glass collecting, washing, and table wiping while the training takes place.

COMMUNICATING

Definition: You're meeting new people or sharing new ideas within or outside your organisation.

The owner and supervisor are COMMUNICATING. The owner shares a new idea and, in doing so, brings the supervisor along on the journey and gives him the opportunity to introduce his own suggestions. The supervisor shares the overall idea with the rest of the staff prior to making the change.

Sharing new ideas or meeting new people can bring new opportunities. It is great practice to bring people along on your journey as they might have a different view or might see something that you have missed. They might even have a better idea.

Other examples:

- Sharing your vision or strategy
- Sharing your ideas for improvement
- Networking within or outside your organisation

The owner and supervisor agree on the new plan and the owner gives the go-ahead to start once everyone is aware of the plan and any concerns have been addressed.

IMPROVING

Definition: You're learning, teaching, or enhancing your organisation, what it does or who it does it with.

By agreeing, the owner is IMPROVING. Not only will the changes improve the experience for customers, they will also improve the glass collector's job.

It's easy to confuse THINKING about an improvement and COMMUNICATING it, with the act of IMPROVING. To improve, a positive change needs to occur. Until that point, it's just an idea and words.

Other examples:

- Teaching as part of a succession plan
- Learning a new skill
- Agreeing to make a positive change

NOTE: There is an important difference between teaching (IMPROVING) and instructing (DIRECTING). Teaching is explaining the desired outcome, explaining why it's important, and participating in a discussion as to how the outcome should be achieved. Instructing is showing someone how to do something by pointing out each of the steps to achieving the desired outcome. The former is far more impactful.

You finish your food, sip the final drops of your drink and leave the bar to think about what you've seen and how it applies to you, your people and your organisation.

The Diary Detox Categories

As a reminder the Diary Detox Categories can be seen together in Figure 1:

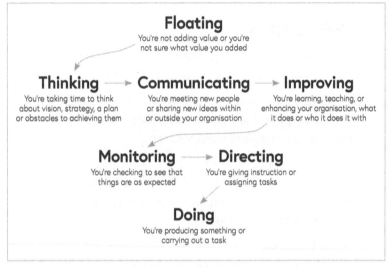

Figure 1 - The Diary Detox Categories

To use the Diary Detox Categories, you will first need to add them into your electronic calendar.

> **ACTION:** Add the Diary Detox Categories to your electronic calendar using the instructions, specific to your electronic calendar, on page 90.
>
> **COME BACK WHEN DONE.**

Each of the Diary Detox Categories, except for FLOATING, are equally important to you and your organisation, but only if they appear in your diary in the appropriate proportion. As you go through your Initial Diary Detox, you'll find out what proportion of each Diary Detox Category will maximise your effectiveness in your role.

One at a time please!

Before you start using the Diary Detox Categories, it's important to point out that each activity in your diary can have assigned only one of the seven Diary Detox Categories: THINKING, COMMUNICATING, IMPROVING, MONITORING, DIRECTING, DOING or FLOATING.

What happens if an activity in your diary is partly COMMUNICATING and partly FLOATING? In that case, you must choose the category that describes the majority of time spent on that activity.

Think back to the story earlier, when the bar owner and supervisor were talking about the new idea. If they met for one hour, with twenty minutes spent discussing the new idea (COMMUNICATING) and forty minutes spent generally chit-chatting (FLOATING), then the majority of the time was spent FLOATING. In that case, FLOATING would be the Diary Detox Category assigned to that activity.

Does that seem harsh? Well, you want time back, right? The only way to get time back is by understanding where most of yours goes and by becoming ruthless with it.

To maximise the value of their time, the bar owner and supervisor could have elected to end the meeting after twenty minutes. All of that time would then have been COMMUNICATING. You have the same choice with every activity you take on.

To select the appropriate Diary Detox Category for any activity, start at the top of Figure 1 (FLOATING) and ask yourself, "Does this category's description match with how the majority of time is spent?".

If it is, that's the category you should use. If not, follow the arrow to the next category, ask the same question and so on. If you manage to reach the bottom Diary Detox Category (DOING), there's no need to ask yourself the question. In that case DOING is correct category.

There's more to this than meets the eye

By grouping the Diary Detox Categories, take a closer look at how they can add even more insight about how you use your time:

LEADING achieves MORE

You might have noticed that you hear the phrase 'bad leader' or 'poor leadership', more and more these days. If the words 'bad' or 'poor' are used anywhere near the word 'leader', then they're not leading at all. Be under no misconception, you're a manager until someone thinks of you as a leader. But, what do you need to do to have those around you think of you as a leader?

To answer this, take a moment to think of someone who you believe is a great leader.

What is it that singles them out as a leader for you? Perhaps they inspire you with their passion to make someone or something better. After all, that's why you follow a leader, because you believe they'll make your world better, right?

But what is it that leaders do to make the world better? Well, first they have an idea, then they explore it with others to make sure it is a good idea and refine it if necessary, and finally they put in place the activities that make the idea a reality. Do these sound familiar?

Thinking	**Communicating**	**Improving**
You're taking time to think about vision, strategy, a plan or obstacles to achieving them	You're meeting new people or sharing new ideas within or outside your organisation	You're learning, teaching, or enhancing your organisation, what it does or who it does it with

Figure 2 - The Diary Detox Leading Categories

Figure 2 shows THINKING, COMMUNICATING and IMPROVING, the fundamental ingredients of LEADING: making the world, and those within it, better.

You might have gone through life up to this point believing that leading is a selfless act, purely for the benefit of others. In fact, leading is as much about making you better as it is about making those around you better.

Don't believe it? Consider the definition of IMPROVING, the last of the Diary Detox Leading Categories in Figure 2:

*"You're **learning**, **teaching**, or **enhancing your organisation**, **what it does or who it does it with.**"*

Take a moment to consider each part of that definition separately:

You're learning

By learning something, you are expanding your mind so that you can apply what you have learned. That is about making *you* better.

You're teaching

In teaching someone, either directly or indirectly by providing them with learning opportunities, you're expanding their mind so that they can apply what they have learned. They might apply what they have learned to your world. Even if they don't, by teaching them, it will help build their trust and loyalty to you. By caring about their development, they'll care about you.

If you're sceptical about that, think about the leader you had in your mind earlier. Despite not receiving any money or reward from them, would you try and help them if they asked? Of course, they're your leader.

Therefore, by teaching someone you're making *your* world better.

You're enhancing your organisation, what it does or who it does it with

By enhancing your organisation, you are making the worlds of those connected to your organisation better. Making the worlds of those connected to your organisation better will build their trust in you and help build their loyalty to you.

By enhancing your organisation, you're making *your* world better.

Therefore, if you spend the appropriate amount of your time LEADING: THINKING, COMMUNICATING and IMPROVING, you will make the worlds of those around you better and you will make your world better too.

MANAGING achieves the SAME

Think about the supervisor in the story earlier. Their primary role was to manage. This meant checking to make sure their customers were happy by ensuring each of the employees in the bar was doing their job. That's MONITORING and DIRECTING, the essence of MANAGING as shown in Figure 3.

Monitoring

You're checking to see that things are as expected

Directing

You're giving instruction or assigning tasks

Figure 3 - The Diary Detox Managing Categories

MANAGING is important but should be done in moderation. If you spend too much of your time MANAGING, you'll have no time left for LEADING. Your world will simply remain the SAME. Sure, your world won't deteriorate, but it won't get better either.

DOING achieves LESS

Every DOING activity you take on is time taken away from MANAGING and LEADING. Therefore, too much DOING will take you, your team or your organisation, backwards. This is because your organisation needs you to use your knowledge and experience for bigger and better things than day to day activities that anyone else could do just as well, if not better.

Doing

You're producing something or
carrying out a task

Figure 4 - The Diary Detox Doing Category

FLOATING achieves NOTHING

A FLOATING activity is an activity where you add no value, or you're not sure what value you add. It shouldn't be surprising that if you allow too many FLOATING activities into your diary you will get nothing. Beware, you can only float for so long before you sink.

Floating

You're not adding value or you're
not sure what value you added

Figure 5 - The Diary Detox Floating Category

Your diary is telling you a story

As you progress through the Diary Detox, you will see how much of your time is allocated to each Diary Detox Category. The proportion of time allocated to each Diary Detox Category will predict if, and how, your world will change in the future.

You'll see if your actions are likely to achieve more, achieve the same, achieve less or achieve nothing. What you do with that insight is entirely up to you.

"I have no choice over the amount of DOING in my diary!"

One of the earliest Diary Detox clients was a senior manager in a medium-sized business. Their desire was to achieve a seat on the company's executive board.

Having completed the Diary Detox, frequent updates on their progress revealed that they were spending the majority of their time DOING with small amounts of time spent MANAGING*. Very little LEADING† was present.

It was reinforced that the predominance of DOING in their diary suggested they would ultimately achieve less. The senior manager emphasised that they had no choice due to budget constraints and continued on the course they had chosen. They had not shared that insight with their own manager and had simply assumed that the budget constraint existed.

Within six months, not only had they not risen to the executive board, but they had also been made redundant.

Had they listened to their diary, they could have used more THINKING, COMMUNICATING and IMPROVING to influence their boss and the board to highlight the impact of the budget constraints and reduce the amount of DOING in their diary.

PART ONE

THE INITIAL DIARY DETOX
WHAT HAVE YOU BEEN DOING?

*"Yesterday is gone.
Tomorrow has not yet come.
We have only today. Let us begin."*

Mother Teresa

Introduction

Before you go on any journey - and getting time back is most definitely a journey - it's important to know two things:

- Where are you now?
- Where are you going?

In the following pages, the Initial Diary Detox will provide the answer to both questions. You'll meet the five Diary Detox Steps: Diary, Evaluate, Target, Opportunity and X-Change - each vital to your Diary Detox journey. You'll turn your diary into a heatmap, a kaleidoscope of colour that will tell you if you are spending your time moving forward, standing still, or sliding backwards. You'll also discover a technique for gaining greater clarity about what you want to achieve, whether you're on track to achieve it and, if not, what's missing.

You will only complete the Initial Diary Detox once. That time is right now.

If you're ready, let's get started with D, for Diary.

Diary - What are you doing?

The Diary step is about finding out how you have spent your time until now. You might think you already know how you spend your time, but it's amazing how many people get to the end of the Diary step in their Initial Diary Detox and say, "I think I can see where my problem is!".

"I didn't realise I was doing so much of that!"

One client, a business coach, spent a significant proportion of time coaching clients. This often involved travelling to and from clients' premises.

Having completed the Initial Diary Detox, the business coach realised how much time he spent travelling to clients, and why he was often late to those meetings - he hadn't planned travel time into his diary.

He then realised that by accepting a meeting into his diary, he not only accepted the time required to attend the meeting. He also implicitly committed to prepare for the meeting, travel to and from it, and carry out any follow-up actions that arose. From that moment, he started to capture the true time required for each meeting.

The aim of the Diary step is for you to have a complete view of all your work-related activities, over the course of one week, both during and outside normal working hours.

First, choose a week from your recent past, one that is representative of your normal working week. If there isn't such a thing as a normal working week for you, don't worry, pick a week that is as typical for you as possible. Your chosen week must be a week where you can remember everything you did that was work-related, absolutely everything.

If you can't find a week where you remember everything, you can still do the Initial Diary Detox. Just read the rest of the Diary step, so that you know what's required, and spend a week recording everything work-related in your electronic diary. That will become your chosen week. At that point, come back and pick up where you left off.

What hours do you want to work?

Now that you have your chosen week, it's time to look at what activity falls within and outside your normal working hours. To do this, you need to answer a question:

What do you want your **normal working hours** to be?

Seriously, this is where you start to take back control of your time. Taking back control starts with you deciding the hours that you want to work. You might have a job that mandates that you work at least 35 hours per week. You might have a job that requires more, or less. Regardless, it's likely that you often work far longer than your contract states. Now you get to decide. What are your minimum contracted hours, and how many hours beyond those do you want to work, if at all?

"I want to work when I choose!"

A business owner struggled with the concept of setting normal working hours. "I don't want to set specific hours. I want to work when I choose!" they said.

Choosing your normal working hours isn't about constraining when you work. It's about creating a basic structure around which you choose to work.

Just because you aim to work between 9am and 5pm every day, it doesn't stop you from working in the evening if that's what you want.

Once you've decided how many hours you want to (or have to) work, decide when you will ideally work those hours. For example, you might work a standard Monday to Friday, 9am to 5pm, or you might flex your hours to create a better work-life balance.

ACTION: Decide on your desired working hours and fill in the table on page 95*, like the table shown in Figure 6 below.

NOTE: If you want to work across two or more sessions in the same day, simply add more than one start and finish time for that day.

COME BACK WHEN DONE.

Day	Start Time	Finish Time
Monday		
Tuesday		
Wednesday		
Thursday		
Friday		
Saturday		
Sunday		

Figure 6 Your desired working hours

What are you doing during your desired working hours?

Now you know your desired working hours, look at your 'chosen week' in your diary. What were you doing during your desired working hours? Your diary should contain meetings that were already arranged. Now you need to fill any empty space in your diary during your desired working hours with everything else that you did.

* or get a copy from
www.diarydetox.com/resources/book

Everything means everything: writing documents, replying to emails, doing expenses, taking phone calls, grabbing coffee or a cigarette, internet shopping, booking a holiday, lunch, travel between meetings, chats with colleagues, phone calls from your partner…everything you did during your desired working hours.

Use a minimum time slot for each activity. Fifteen or thirty minutes is a realistic minimum time slot. However, choose whatever minimum time slot is suitable for your organisation or profession.

ACTION: For your desired working hours, fill the gaps between what's already in your diary with everything else that you did.

COME BACK WHEN DONE.

What are you doing outside your desired working hours?

To ensure that you get a complete view of how work has been creeping into your personal time, you also need to include work-related activity that happens outside your desired working hours.

For example, say you spent 20 minutes looking at your emails on Sunday evening (and let's also assume that Sunday evening isn't part of your desired working hours), put that in your diary.

ACTION: Include in your diary all work-related activity outside your desired working hours.

COME BACK WHEN DONE.

That's D done!

Honestly, that's it, you've completed the first step of your Initial Diary Detox.

You should now have a week in your diary showing an accurate view of all activity during your desired working hours and showing what work-related activity crept into your personal time outside those hours.

ACTION: Take a few moments to reflect on what fills your diary in an average week. Note down your thoughts on the following:

How many hours do you actually spend working during the average week?

What do you spend most of your time doing?

What surprises you?

Now you know exactly what you spent your time doing during your chosen week, it's time to find out the value of that time.

E is for Evaluate.

Evaluate – What value are you adding?

Knowing what you do is one thing but understanding the value it adds is another. If you already go to meetings, no doubt you expect them to be worth attending. After all, you wouldn't go to a meeting expecting it to be a waste of time, would you? In fact, losing time attending unnecessary meetings happens more often than you'd think, but frequently you don't realise it.

The Evaluate step will help you to reflect and ask whether you spent your time adding value?

Using the secret sauce

The Evaluate step is where you get to use the Diary Detox Categories, that you were introduced to earlier, for the first time. As a reminder they are repeated in Figure 7.

Figure 7 - The Diary Detox Categories

> **ACTION:** Go through each activity in your chosen week
> and categorise it using the Diary Detox Categories, see
> Figure 7.
>
> **COME BACK WHEN DONE.**

That's E done!

Well done, you're flying along. You now know what you spent your time doing and the value of each activity. Your diary should be full of activities for your chosen week, each evaluated using one of the Diary Detox Categories. In the Target step, you'll add colour to each Diary Detox Category. For now, every activity in your chosen week should have the same neutral colour.

> **ACTION:** Take a few moments to reflect on the value of
> the activities in your diary for your chosen week:
>
> What surprises you?

You're done with your diary for now. Close it and put it to one side. Don't worry, you'll come back to it shortly. Now it's time to consider how you *should* be spending your time.

T is for Target.

Target – What should you be doing?

So far, you've looked at what activities fill your diary and the value they provide. In the Target step you'll find out what you *should* be doing with your time.

If you're saying to yourself, "I know what I should be doing" then you're not alone. You're like many others who have said the same while going through the Diary Detox journey. More often than not, having completed the Target step of the Initial Diary Detox, the reaction from those same people is, "Wow, I've never thought of my role that way before!". Some even changed part of their role after realising something was missing altogether.

Find your targets

Targets are things you want to achieve by a specific time in the future. What time in the future is up to you, but it's important to have a specific time in mind. It could be next week, next month, next quarter or even next year. It should be a point by which you want to achieve a number of outcomes that will contribute to a significant milestone. That milestone might be, for example, a promotion deadline, a cut-off date for sales targets, or the financial year end.

> **ACTION:** Think about a timeframe for your role by which you want to achieve a significant milestone.
>
> **COME BACK WHEN DONE.**

Next, to help you identify the targets that will contribute to you achieving that significant milestone, think about the person, or people, to whom you feel most accountable in terms of achieving that milestone. They could be your boss, your manager, shareholders, your life partner or your business buddy. It doesn't really matter who they are. It only matters that you care deeply about their perception of your achievements.

> **ACTION:** Think about the person, or people, to whom you are most accountable in terms of achieving your milestone.
>
> **COME BACK WHEN DONE.**

Imagine sitting in front of that person (or people, if you have thought of more than one) on the day of your significant milestone. Imagine telling them that you have arrived at your milestone having just smashed your targets. They smile and ask what you've achieved.

What would you want to be able to say that would convince them that you had smashed your targets?

> **ACTION:** Write each of your targets in the table on page 96*, like the table shown in Figure 8.
>
> While you have space for ten targets, try to start with four or five. If you add more, you risk adding activities rather than targets. The remaining spaces can be used later if you find something you missed. Use a pencil just in case you want to change your targets later.
>
> Don't worry about the columns with the headings 'Who?' and 'In Diary?' yet. You'll use those shortly.
>
> HINT: If you have no idea where to start identifying targets, look at your job description or objectives.
>
> **COME BACK WHEN DONE.**

* or get a copy from
www.diarydetox.com/resources/book

Who?	Target	In Diary?

Figure 8 Diary Detox Targets

You now have the first draft of your Diary Detox Targets. Here's a technique to make sure you've covered everything.

Now Imagine that you are the person to whom you are most accountable. You've just listened to someone say they've smashed their targets. If they showed you the targets in your Diary Detox Targets table, would you think that they had smashed them?

ACTION: If you don't think they would have smashed their targets, add or change the targets as necessary and keep repeating this step until you're happy.

COME BACK WHEN DONE.

You now have your final set of Diary Detox Targets and therefore know what you are accountable for getting done by your target date.

Who should be responsible for each target?

While you are accountable for ensuring your targets are hit, you are not necessarily responsible for carrying them out. To decide this, you'll need Figure 9 below:

Figure 9 - Diary Detox Responsibilities

What do 3, 2 and 1 mean?

3 means that you are accountable for the target and have delegated (or will delegate) responsibility and therefore won't do it yourself.

2 means you are responsible for that target and will do it yourself at the moment because there is no one else available who can be delegated to. Be mindful when deciding whether to assign a 2, consider this question: If there were someone else available who knows what you know, could do what you do, whom you could trust without question, but who doesn't have your job title, would you be comfortable giving this target to them? If the answer is yes, then assign a 2.

1 means that you are both accountable and responsible for the target and will do it yourself, because it's at the core of your role. Without such tasks you wouldn't have a role.

> **ACTION:** For each target in your Diary Detox Targets table, use Figure 9 to fill in the 'Who?' column with the number that represents your role in that target.
>
> **COME BACK WHEN DONE.**

Ideal world

In an ideal world, your Diary Detox Targets should have mostly 3s (you've delegated as much as possible), zero 2s (you're doing nothing that someone else should be doing), and few 1s (focussed personal responsibility for as little as possible).

Don't worry if you have lots of 2s and 1s and not enough 3s right now, that's why you're reading this book. To get close to the ideal world will require THINKING, COMMUNICATING and IMPROVING, but you'll get into that later.

Let's add some colour to this picture

Now that you have a clear and complete understanding of your targets and your role in achieving them, you're close to seeing the value you get from your time by assigning colours to the Diary Detox Categories in your diary.

The mix of colours you will see will immediately reveal how far your current activities reflect those of someone operating successfully at your level of seniority.

Each Diary Detox Category is assigned to one of the colours as follows:

Thinking
You're taking time to think about vision, strategy, a plan or obstacles to achieving them

Communicating
You're meeting new people or sharing new ideas within or outside your organisation

Improving
You're learning, teaching, or enhancing your organisation, what it does or who it does it with

Figure 10 - The Leading Categories (Green)

Monitoring
You're checking to see that things are as expected

Directing
You're giving instruction or assigning tasks

Figure 11 - The Managing Categories (Amber)

Doing
You're producing something or carrying out a task

Figure 12 - The Doing Category (Red)

Floating
You're not adding value or you're not sure what value you added

Figure 13 - The Floating Category (Brown)

Before you add the colours, it's a good idea to consider what mix of colours should you expect to see?

The Diary Detox Role Ratios in Figure 14 represent the ideal balance of activities, in an average week, for people operating at different levels of seniority within an organisation.

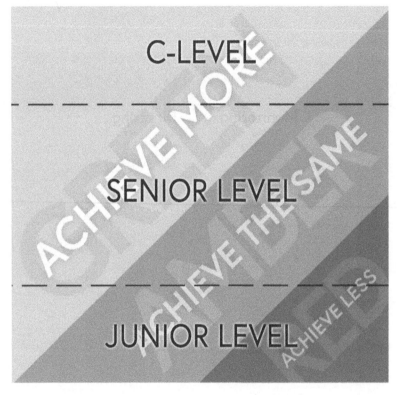

Figure 14 - Diary Detox Role Ratios

Based upon the average five-day working week, 20% represents a day of your time.

Therefore, C-level managers should expect to spend approximately four days a week (80%) on GREEN activities, and one day a week (20%) on AMBER activities and no RED activity (DOING).

Are you wondering how C-level managers are supposed to have no RED activity (DOING) when RED activity includes travel? Does that mean that C-level managers shouldn't travel? Not at all. With a little creative thinking there's always a way to turn any activity from one colour to another. While C-level managers will spend some of their time travelling, they can always use that time for other activities. For example, listening to an educational podcast while travelling will help turn RED time into GREEN time (IMPROVING) as they will be learning as they travel.

You'll notice that BROWN doesn't appear in the Diary Detox Role Ratios at all. FLOATING activity is not ideal for anyone who wants to be successful, at any level.

It's time to decide which section of Figure 14 you sit in (see the dotted horizontal lines). Where you sit determines what colour mix you should expect to see in your electronic diary for your chosen week once the colours have been turned-on.

Finding where you fit

C-Level managers: business owners, managing directors, board members and those in what's commonly known as the C-Suite (CEO, COO, CIO, CMO etc.) sit in the top section.

Senior managers: executive directors, senior directors, divisional heads, etc. sit in the middle section.

Junior managers sit in the bottom section.

These groupings are a guideline only. You have complete freedom to place yourself in any section of the Diary Detox Role Ratios you choose.

In many industries, you will only achieve promotion when you are operating at the level you aspire to. Therefore, if you are looking to step up to a more senior level, you might want to place yourself at the level you want to achieve.

NOTE: If you are a business owner and your business contains only you right now, your Diary Detox Role Ratio is likely represented by the whole square because you are filling the roles of C-level, senior and junior manager all at the same time. Therefore, you should expect to be spending about 50% of your time on GREEN activities, about 30% of your time on AMBER activities and 20% of your time on RED activities.

ACTION: Based on where you have chosen to sit in the Diary Detox Roles Ratio diagram, write down the proportion of GREEN, AMBER and RED that you want to see in the table on page 95*, like the table shown in Figure 15.

COME BACK WHEN DONE.

Colour	Percentage or Days (per week)
GREEN (LEADING)	
AMBER (MANAGING)	
RED (DOING)	

Figure 15 Desired Diary Detox Ratio

The big reveal

This is it; this is where you add some colour to your diary and find out how you currently spend your time.

Do you see the colour mix you expect? Don't worry if you don't, that's what you're here to address. Regardless of how the colours turned out for you, your diary is now a mirror, reflecting how you spend your time. As you continue through the Diary Detox, you will learn tools that will help you achieve your desired colour mix and the results that you want.

ACTION: Take a moment to reflect. Ask yourself the following:

What colour mix did you expect?
GREEN (LEADING) -
AMBER (MANAGING) -
RED (DOING) -
BROWN (FLOATING) -

What colour mix did you see?
GREEN (LEADING) -
AMBER (MANAGING) -
RED (DOING) -
BROWN (FLOATING) -

Did anything surprise you?

The colours have another use

The colours you now see in your diary can help you make decisions, as well as show you the amount of LEADING, MANAGING, DOING and FLOATING present in your diary.

Suppose you need to make space and remove something from your diary urgently, how do you know which activity to remove? The colours in your diary will give you a clue.

GREEN means 'go'

When your body is under stress, it begins to prepare for fight or flight by producing Cortisol. One of the effects of Cortisol is to shut down any non-essential systems in your body. In that moment, your body simply needs to survive, so one of the things it shuts down is growth, as a short-term response. You can do the same with your diary.

GREEN represents LEADING activity that results in making things better, growth.

When your diary comes under stress, it's important that you survive. For a short period, you don't need to grow. Therefore, if you choose not to do a GREEN activity, it means something might not improve in the short-term, but at least you'll survive to see another day.

So, if you need to make space in your diary urgently, and unexpectedly, you can remove a GREEN activity.

NOTE: If you choose to remove GREEN activities for a prolonged period, perhaps due to lengthy periods of unexpected interruptions, this will spell the death of growth. Aim to keep periods of non-growth to an absolute minimum.

AMBER means 'warning'

AMBER represents MANAGING and is all about making sure things are being done as expected. AMBER is a warning colour. If you choose not to do an AMBER activity, be warned, it means an activity won't be checked or might not be acted upon if it's failing.

RED means 'stop'

RED represents DOING activities that produce something or carry out a core task. RED is the colour of danger. If you choose not to do a RED activity, be very careful, it means the activity won't be carried out or something won't be produced.

BROWN means 'rubbish'

No one needs or wants waste. Wherever you see BROWN in your diary, you can be sure that it can be removed without consequence.

That's T done!

You now know what you have spent your time doing, the value of your activities and how much of your time is spent LEADING, MANAGING, DOING and FLOATING.

You also know how you compare to your ideal colour mix and know the targets you want to achieve.

The next question is, how much of what you *should* be doing to achieve your targets have you *actually* been doing?

O is for Opportunity.

Opportunity – What's missing from your diary?

If you spend all of your time at work on activities that contribute nothing to the success of your organisation, you'd expect to achieve very little. Believe it or not, this might be happening to you right now without you realising it.

The Opportunity step is a very short and incredibly powerful step that will tell you if you've have fallen into the complacency trap.

One very simple question

The key to the Opportunity step is to ask one simple question. You'll need your Diary Detox Targets from page 96* and your chosen week in your electronic diary for this activity.

ACTION: For each of your Diary Detox Targets, look at your chosen week in your diary and ask yourself, 'Are ALL the activities required to achieve that target by the target date, present in your chosen week?'

If the answer is 'YES', put a tick in the column headed 'In Diary?'.

If the answer is 'NO', put a cross in the column headed 'In Diary?.

Move to the next target and repeat until you have put a tick or cross next to each of your Diary Detox Targets.

COME BACK WHEN DONE.

You should now have a tick or cross next to each of your Diary Detox Targets. Each cross represents a target that will likely be missed if you continue on the same course.

That's O done!

That's the Opportunity step done. You now know which targets have activity missing from your chosen week in your diary.

ACTION: Take a moment to reflect.

What, if anything, surprised you?

The next and final step of the Initial Diary Detox will help you consider what activities were missing from your chosen week that would have achieved those targets.

X is for X-change.

X-Change – What should you do differently?

You're nearing the end of your Initial Diary Detox. The Opportunity step showed you which of your Diary Detox Targets were at risk of not being delivered.

To make sure those targets are delivered going forward, you need to create a list of what was missing from your chosen week. The X-Change step will help you create that list.

NOTE: You will need a piece of notepaper for this step.

ACTION: Look at your Diary Detox Targets on page 96* and find the first target that has a cross next to it in the 'In Diary?' column.

Write the name of that target as a heading on your piece of notepaper and, underneath, write the answer to the following question:

'What activities were missing from your chosen week that would have allowed you to put a tick next to this target instead of a cross?'

Once you have written the missing activities under the heading, change the cross next to that target into a tick.

Repeat for each target that has a cross next to it.

COME BACK WHEN DONE.

That's X done!

You should now have a tick next to each of your Diary Detox Targets and a list of activities that were missing from your chosen week. If those activities are included in your diary going forward, you know you'll be on track to deliver all of your targets.

Keep that list safe, as you'll need to refer back to it during the Weekly Diary Detox.

Your Initial Diary Detox is Done!

Congratulations! You've completed your Initial Diary Detox.

You have been introduced to the five Diary Detox steps: Diary, Evaluate, Target, Opportunity and X-Change. You have also been introduced to the Diary Detox Categories and their associated colours, the Diary Detox Targets, and the Diary Detox Role Ratios.

You have practiced using each of these tools and have had the chance to reflect on how you've spent your time until now.

Having completed the Initial Diary Detox, you now know:

- What you have been doing. (Diary step)

- What value it brings. (Evaluate step)

- What you need to achieve. (Target step)

- What proportion of your time is spent LEADING, MANAGING, DOING and FLOATING. (Target step)

- How you spend your time compared to others at your level who are successful. (Target step)

- Which of your desired targets were unlikely to be met. (Opportunity step)

- Which activities were missing from your diary. (X-change step)

ACTION: Take a moment to reflect.

What did you learn about yourself, your diary and your time?

Now that you've completed the Initial Diary Detox you're in the perfect position to start the Weekly Diary Detox, a weekly activity that will keep you on track to deliver your targets and save you a day in your diary, every week. Everything you have read and done so far in this book has been to prepare you for this moment.

PART TWO

THE WEEKLY DIARY DETOX
GETTING INTO THE HABIT

"We are what we repeatedly do. Excellence, then, is not an act, but a habit."

Will Durant

Introduction

The Weekly Diary Detox is the single most important habit for you to get into in order to disrupt and improve your relationship with time. It is a weekly activity, lasting up to thirty minutes, that will ensure your diary is detoxed going forward.

In your Weekly Diary Detox, you will use the five Diary Detox steps: Diary, Evaluate, Target, Opportunity and X-change, to reflect on your diary for the past week, and to make sure your coming week contains all the activities you need to meet your Diary Detox Targets. The Weekly Diary Detox will also ensure that the rest of your time (yes, there might be time left over) is focused on adding value to you and your organisation.

After the first few weeks, your Weekly Diary Detox should take no longer than thirty minutes. Eventually, with the help of some handy tips, which you will find later in this chapter, your Weekly Diary Detox can take as little as five minutes. That's a small price to pay for your peace of mind as you head into your downtime.

Habits take 66 days to form

It takes sixty-six days (just over two months) for a new habit to form[*] This is important. If you make the Weekly Diary Detox a habit, you will be more productive and effective than you have ever been. Get out of the habit and you risk undoing the progress you've made.

As the name suggests, the Weekly Diary Detox is a weekly activity. To help the habit form, you should plan it into your diary now.

Schedule the Weekly Diary Detox as close to the end of your week as possible, but not so close that you're too tired to do it. Avoid last thing at the end of your working week.

Also, find a time that is unlikely to get overbooked or interrupted.

---

* Lally, van Jaarsveld, Potts, Wardle: 'How habits are formed: Modelling habit formation in the real world', July 2009.

First thing in the morning on the last day of your working week is a great option. For most, that might be Friday morning.

If you work Monday to Friday you might be wondering, 'Why not do my Weekly Diary Detox first thing Monday morning?'.

Imagine that you finish work on Friday, having NOT done your Weekly Diary Detox. You haven't planned out your next week and that might play on your mind and hinder your ability to relax for the weekend. In addition, imagine that something critical happens over the weekend or on Monday morning, requiring your immediate attention. By the time you get around to your Weekly Diary Detox, your week is in full swing and you've missed the opportunity to get full value out of your week.

> **ACTION:** Insert a weekly recurring appointment into your electronic diary called, 'Weekly Diary Detox' and categorise it as MONITORING.
>
> **COME BACK WHEN DONE.**

Your Weekly Diary Detox is about making sure that your week contains everything that it should, and that you get the most from your time. This is MONITORING, an AMBER activity. Therefore, if you choose not to do your Weekly Diary Detox, you'll potentially miss one of your Diary Detox Targets.

Simply follow the steps

The steps in the Weekly Diary Detox have been made short and simple. To help you save time and stay on track, the steps have been brought together in the form of a checklist on page 94, just like the list in Figure 16.

Diary	Ensure everything you did **this** week is in your diary Ensure **next** week's commitments are in your diary	☐ ☐
Evaluate	Ensure this week's categories are still correct Categorise all of next week's activities	☐ ☐
Target	Review your Targets and change if necessary Erase the ticks from the 'In Diary' column	☐ ☐
Opportunity	Tick or cross 'In Diary' for each target depending on whether present in **next** weeks Diary	☐
X-change	In 1, 2, 3 order, insert and activity in your diary for each target with a cross and tick when inserted	☐
	Reflect on your colour mix against Roles Ratios Fill remaining space with 'green' activities	☐ ☐

Figure 16 - The Weekly Diary Detox Checklist

In this chapter, we will go through each step on the checklist in detail. A rough estimate of the time required to complete each step is included. You can come back to this chapter to help you complete the checklist each week until you're well-practised at it.

As you complete each item in the checklist, put a tick next to it in the box provided and move on.

Are you ready to make sure your diary contains everything you need next week to deliver all your targets? If so, then you're ready for your Weekly Diary Detox.

As with everything Diary Detox, you'll start with D for Diary.

Diary (approx. 5 mins)

Ensure everything you did this week is in your diary

Change is inevitable. You'll be interrupted, or you might simply change your mind about what is important. Since the Weekly Diary Detox is partly about helping you to reflect on your past week, your diary needs to reflect what you actually did. The first part of the Diary step makes sure your diary matches exactly what you did in the past week regardless of what you had planned.

NOTE: If this is your first Weekly Diary Detox, you can skip this action box because you already completed the action as part of your Initial Diary Detox.

ACTION: If you didn't attend a meeting or complete an activity that was scheduled in your diary in the **past week**, move (or remove) it and insert what you actually did at that time.

Also, if there is blank space in your diary during your desired working hours for the past week, fill it with what you did during that time.

COME BACK WHEN DONE.

Ensure next week's commitments are in your diary

If you look at next week in your diary you should see activities that have already been scheduled. For example, you might see meetings to which you have been invited, and meetings where you are the organiser. Now you need to add all other predictable commitments for the coming week.

"I'm only supposed to work four days a week!"

A Director of Sales and Marketing had an agreement with their company that required them to work only four days per week. Despite this, they had never managed to actually work a four-day week in the three months they had held their role.

As part of the Diary step within their Weekly Diary Detox, they started to block-out the day where they were not supposed to be in the office. Still, they believed that they would not have enough time to get everything done without the extra day.

Completing each of the Diary Detox steps showed them that they not only had the time to achieve all their targets, but they also had time to spare, even with their day off included.

> **ACTION:** Insert activities that you can predict in your **coming week**. Don't worry about inserting activity for your Diary Detox Targets yet as they will be covered in the X-Change step, later.
>
> Examples of things you might add:
>
> - Regular days off.
> - Lunch every day (seriously, put it in now).
> - Travel to and from meetings.
> - Preparation and follow-up time for meetings.
> - Regular coffees / chats that you tend to have.
>
> **COME BACK WHEN DONE.**

That's D done!

Reviewing last week's diary and planning this week should have taken approximately five minutes. You now have a complete view of what you actually did last week and of what you are already committed to for the coming week.

Evaluate (approx. 5 mins)

Ensure this week's categories are still correct

When you create activities or accept meetings in your diary, you make a judgement about which Diary Detox Category applies. With the best will in the world, things often don't turn out as you expect.

For example, a meeting with a client might end up being a complete waste of time, or a request for help might in fact be an attempt by a colleague to get you to do their work for them. A meeting that you arrange might go horribly wrong and result in all the attendees walking out of the room muttering, 'Well there's an hour I'm never getting back in my life'.

It's not a problem, it's part of life. But when it happens you need to know and consider why it happened and how you can avoid it happening again.

Part of the Evaluate step is about reflecting on whether each the activities in your past week added the value you expected. If they didn't, you should change the Diary Detox Category to reflect the value the activities provided (better or worse).

A reminder of the Diary Detox Categories can be found in Figure 17. For each diary activity, simply select the category description that represents how the majority of your time was spent.

Floating
You're not adding value or you're not sure what value you added

Thinking
You're taking time to think about vision, strategy, a plan or obstacles to achieving them

Communicating
You're meeting new people or sharing new ideas within or outside your organisation

Improving
You're learning, teaching, or enhancing your organisation, what it does or who it does it with

Monitoring
You're checking to see that things are as expected

Directing
You're giving instruction or assigning tasks

Doing
You're producing something or carrying out a task

Figure 17 - The Diary Detox Categories (with arrows and colour)

NOTE: If this is your first Weekly Diary Detox, you can skip this action because you completed the action as part of your Initial Diary Detox.

> **ACTION:** For each activity in your **past week** make sure the Diary Detox Category is still correct. If it isn't, change the category to reflect the actual value the activity provided.
>
> **COME BACK WHEN DONE.**

Categorise all of next week's activities

It's important to understand what value you expect from each of the activities in your coming week.

> **ACTION:** For each of the activities in your diary for **next week**, categorise them using the Diary Detox Categories.
>
> **COME BACK WHEN DONE.**

That's E done!

The Evaluate step should have taken approximately five minutes. All activity for the past week and next week should now have the appropriate Diary Detox Category assigned.

Target (approx. 5 mins)

Review your targets and change if necessary

From week to week, your targets can change. You might be given more responsibility; you might complete one of your existing targets and no longer need to track it; you might simply realise that something was missing; or you might delegate responsibility for a particular task that you were previously responsible for yourself.

The Target step is where you make sure your Diary Detox Targets are still correct. You'll need your Diary Detox Targets table on page 96* for this.

ACTION: Remove any targets from your Diary Detox Targets table that have now been achieved or delivered.

COME BACK WHEN DONE.

ACTION: Amend any targets that have changed, either because the description of the target, or the number (1, 2 or 3) within the column headed 'Who?', has changed.

COME BACK WHEN DONE.

Imagine you are now the person to whom you are most accountable. You've just listened to someone say they've smashed their targets. If they showed you the targets in your Diary Detox Targets table, would you think that they had smashed their targets?

> **ACTION:** If not, add whatever is necessary to smash your targets by the target date.
>
> **COME BACK WHEN DONE.**

Erase the ticks from the 'In Diary?' column

You will have used the column headed, 'In Diary?' within the Diary Detox Targets table as part of any previous Weekly Diary Detox and will use them again in this step.

> **ACTION:** Remove the ticks, from the column with the heading 'In Diary?' in the Diary Detox Targets table.
>
> **COME BACK WHEN DONE.**

That's T done!

The Target step should have taken no longer than 5 minutes and you now know that your Diary Detox Targets are up to date.

Opportunity (approx. 5 mins)

In this step, you will find out if the activities required to deliver each of your targets are included in your coming week.

You will need your Diary Detox Targets table on page 96.

Tick or cross 'In Diary?' for each target depending on whether it's present in next week's diary

ACTION: Look at each of your targets and decide if the coming week in your diary contains all the activities required to deliver that target by the target date.

If it does, add a tick in the column headed 'In Diary?' and move on. It if doesn't, add a cross in the column headed 'In Diary?' and move on.

NOTE: Don't be tempted to insert any missing activities at this point. You'll be able to take care of that in the next step, X-Change.

COME BACK WHEN DONE.

That's O done!

The Opportunity step should have taken no longer than 5 minutes and you now know what is missing from your diary next week to achieve each of your targets.

X-Change (approximately 10 minutes)

The X-Change step will ensure that the coming week in your diary contains all the activities required to deliver your Diary Detox Targets by the target date, that all remaining space is filled with activities that add value and that you reflect on the colour mix in your coming week.

In 1, 2, 3 order, insert an activity in your diary for each Target with a cross and tick when inserted.

Using your Diary Detox Targets, you're going to ensure that each activity required to deliver your targets, by the target date, is present in your diary.

NOTE: During the X-change step of your Initial Diary Detox you created a list of missing activities. This is where you should refer to them.

You want to ensure that space is allocated first to activities that ONLY YOU should do. Those are the activities with a '1' in the 'Who?' column.

ACTION: If there is one, find the first target with a cross in the 'In Diary?' column and a '1' in the 'Who?' column.

Insert the activities required to ensure that the target is delivered on time.

Once all the required activities are in your diary, change the cross to a tick.

Repeat for the remaining targets with a cross in the 'In Diary?' column and a '1' in the 'Who?' column.

COME BACK WHEN DONE.

Next, you'll allocate time to activities that you do because no one else is available right now. Those are the Diary Detox Targets with a '2' in the 'Who?' column.

ACTION: If there is one, find the first target with a cross in the 'In Diary?' column and a '2' in the 'Who?' column.

Insert the activities required to ensure that the target is delivered on time.

Once all the required activities are in your diary, change the cross to a tick.

Repeat for the remaining targets with a cross in the 'In Diary?' column and a '2' in the 'Who?' column.

COME BACK WHEN DONE.

Finally, you'll allocate MONITORING time to the activities that you have delegated. These are the Diary Detox Targets with a '3' in the 'Who?' column.

ACTION: If there is one, find the first target with a cross in the 'In Diary?' column and a '3' in the 'Who?' column.

Insert the activities required to ensure that the target is delivered on time.

Once all the required activities are in your diary, change the cross to a tick.

Repeat for the remaining targets with a cross in the 'In Diary?' column and a '3' in the 'Who?' column.

COME BACK WHEN DONE.

What if there's no space left to insert any activities?

If, when trying to insert activities, you find you have run out of space, here are a few suggestions that might help.

1. Look for FLOATING activities and remove them.

2. Look for DOING activities. If they don't help you to achieve your targets, why are you doing them? Give them to someone else and remove them from your diary.

3. Look for DOING activities. If they help you to achieve your targets but could be done by someone else, why are you doing them? Give them to someone else, add a MONITORING activity to check progress, and remove them from your diary.

4. Look for MONITORING and DIRECTING activities and see if they are part of your targets. If not, give the activities to someone else and remove them from your diary. If the activities are part of your targets and there are a number of them with the same person, see if you can combine those into a single shorter MONITORING activity.

5. If you have delegated as much as possible and it's the sheer volume of MONITORING activity that is consuming your diary, consider why so much time is needed for MONITORING. This could be a great subject to discuss with your manager, a mentor or coach.

6. If you have delegated as much as possible and you are out of space in your diary, is there a possibility that you have simply too many accountabilities for one person to handle (too many targets)? A coach will be able to help you with this. If you don't have a coach, perhaps speak with your line manager, a mentor, a trusted colleague or a friend. They might be able to identify areas where you can re-assign some of your targets. If the prospect of giving away targets worries you, remember that it's better to succeed at everything in your targets than fail at some.

The list of suggestions above is a logical approach to dealing with too much work in your diary. By following each of the steps, it's likely that your coach, mentor, manager or colleagues might be able to offer suggestions that you may have missed. If you choose to ask them, remember to use your diary, the Diary Detox Categories and colours to explain what's going on in your diary.

Fill remaining space with 'GREEN' activity

The GREEN activities THINKING, COMMUNICATING and IMPROVING ultimately lead to making your world better, so if you have space left in your diary at this point, why wouldn't you fill any space with GREEN activities?

Why not leave the space empty?

If you leave space in your diary empty, it's highly likely that you will use the time for whatever presents itself at that moment, which might not always be the best use of your time. Empty space might result in procrastination, reading emails, or allowing yourself to be interrupted because you have nothing better to do.

Having your available space filled with GREEN activity helps you make the most from the Spot Diary Detox that you will be introduced to later as you will be comparing any unexpected interruption with an activity that is focused on improvement.

What GREEN activity should you fill space with?

It's your choice. If nothing obvious comes to mind, simply put in some THINKING time to start with. If you don't know what to think about, here are some ideas:

- Look at the targets on your Diary Detox Targets table on page 96 with a '2' in the 'Who?' column and think about how you could start to delegate them.

- Talk to your team, colleagues, or customers and get their opinion on what's working and what's not working within your team or organisation.

- Go for a walk outside the office, grab a coffee and just wander. It's amazing what ideas come to mind when you stop actively thinking about work.

Doesn't that mean your diary will be completely full?

Yes, it does and that's the plan.

Won't that mean people have trouble booking meetings with you?

Yes, they will. That's how the Diary Detox works.

Every time someone tries to book your time for a meeting, they'll need to compete for your time. You'll compare and decide whether their meeting justifies moving (or removing) what's already in your diary.

Someone else's request will need to be pretty important to outweigh your GREEN activity.

By making others justify their request for your time, it sends a signal that you respect your time. Others then start to respect your time too.

ACTION: If you have space left in your diary at this point, fill it with GREEN activity: THINKING, COMMUNICATING or IMPROVING.

COME BACK WHEN DONE.

Reflect on your colour mix against the Role Ratios

It is always a good idea to keep an eye on how the colours in your diary compare to your desired percentages.

> **ACTION:** Have a look at the percentage of GREEN, AMBER, RED and BROWN activity in your coming week. Compare and reflect upon how it compares to your desired colour mix in the table on page 95.
>
> **COME BACK WHEN DONE.**

While you may not change anything in your diary as a result of that reflection, any insights would be a great topic of conversation with your manager, a coach or mentor. Seriously, discussing why the mix of colours in your diary differs from your desired percentages will be gold dust to them, since it provides a specific view of how you use your time and your current approach to LEADING, MANAGING and DOING.

Your Weekly Diary Detox is Done!

Congratulations! You've completed your Weekly Diary Detox.

You took the time to reflect on the activities in your past week and the value those activities brought. You also ensured that you fully understand what you need to include in your coming week to be successful, that you included it, and that you filled any remaining time with activity that is focused on improvement. Finally, you saw what proportion of your time was spent LEADING, MANAGING, DOING and FLOATING and how you compare to others at your level who are successful.

Daily habits that will speed up your Weekly Diary Detox

Here are some habits that you can use every day that will significantly speed up your Weekly Diary Detox and allow you to identify potential problems with your time early on.

Change your diary as you change your mind

If you decide to do something different from what you have planned in your diary, change it straightaway. Go to your diary and add, move or remove activity as it happens. In doing so, you will get a head start on the Diary step of your Weekly Diary Detox.

Categorise as things come into your diary

As soon as you put something in your diary, categorise it using the Diary Detox Categories. It's a great habit to assign value to every meeting. Consciously considering the Diary Detox Category can result in you rejecting meeting requests before they are accepted. By doing this, you will also reduce (even remove) the time required for part of the Evaluate step for your Weekly Diary Detox.

Re-categorise as you finish an activity

As you walk out of a meeting, or finish an activity, think about the value you got from it. If it's different from what you expected, re-categorise the activity in your diary straightaway to give yourself a head start on the Evaluate step for your Weekly Diary Detox.

What's next?

Having completed your Weekly Diary Detox you can head home for some downtime and relax, confident in the knowledge that everything you need to do, next week, will be in your diary waiting for you when you come back to work.

Fast forward to the beginning of your next week. You've had a relaxing break with friends and family. As you arrive at the office, not everything is going to plan, or a colleague grabs you for some help. Your diary is in danger of going off-track already. How are you going to manage the situation?

Enter the Spot Diary Detox.

PART THREE

THE SPOT DIARY DETOX
KNOWING WHEN TO SAY 'NO'

> "The major problem of life is learning how to handle the costly interruptions. The door that slams shut, the plan that got side-tracked, the marriage that failed. Or that lovely poem that didn't get written because someone knocked on the door."

Martin Luther King Jr.

Introduction

Having completed your Weekly Diary Detox, you will have a completely full diary that includes all activities you need to deliver your Diary Detox Targets. You might also have a smattering of GREEN activity designed to give you a head start on making yourself, your team and your organisation better. A perfect situation, right? Maybe, but as we all know, not everything always goes to plan.

What if something unexpectedly lands on your plate?

What if a major incident happens that requires your immediate attention?

What if you're interrupted by one of your team, a colleague, a peer, or even someone senior to you in your organisation and you find it hard to say 'no' to people's demands on your time?

This is where the Spot Diary Detox comes in. It's designed to help you deal with unexpected interruptions by applying the five Diary Detox steps in less than 30-seconds. The Spot Diary Detox will interrupt your natural instinct to make a snap decision about your time and will instead get you to ask a few simple questions that ensure you make the right decision about your time in the moment.

The Spot Diary Detox doesn't tell you what to do. You always have the final say over what gets into your diary and what you do with your time. The Spot Diary Detox simply gives you all the information you need to make the right decision, for you, in the moment.

Let's see the Spot Diary Detox in action. You'll need a piece of notepaper for this activity until you get the hang of using it.

Imagine someone interrupts you or something unexpected arises that will potentially impact your diary:

Diary

ACTION: Look at the colour of the activity that's already in your diary (and is in danger of being replaced).

NOTE: If the activity doesn't have a Diary Detox Category, decide it now.

On your piece of notepaper, write down, "I am considering replacing an activity that is [CURRENT COLOUR]".

COME BACK WHEN DONE.

Evaluate

ACTION: Using the Diary Detox Categories, what is the colour of the new activity that you have been interrupted by?

NOTE: If you don't know the Diary Detox Category, you probably don't know enough about the interruption. Ask more questions of the person interrupting you until you know.

On your piece of notepaper, underneath the last statement you wrote, write down, "with an activity that is [NEW COLOUR]"

COME BACK WHEN DONE.

Target

ACTION: Is the new activity going to contribute to you achieving any of your Diary Detox Targets?

On your piece of notepaper, underneath the last statement you wrote, write down, "and that [IS / IS NOT] contributing to my targets."

COME BACK WHEN DONE.

Opportunity

ACTION: Read what you have written so far and choose your response:

- Do it (now or later)
- Delegate it
- Don't do it at all

Remember, it's your choice.

COME BACK WHEN DONE.

X-change

Once you've made your choice, it time to act on it using one of three approaches:

Option one: Do it (now or later)

> **ACTION:** Insert the new activity in your diary and move whatever was in its place and notify those who need to know about your decision.
>
> **COME BACK WHEN DONE.**

Ensure you make the new activity as GREEN as possible.

How do you make an activity as GREEN as possible?

Your instinct may be to accept the new activity by inserting a DOING activity (RED) in your diary.

You could try to make a RED activity AMBER by DIRECTING a colleague, telling them what to do, thereby getting them to do it while you watch.

Better still, consider the possibility of making the activity GREEN by IMPROVING the colleague who has interrupted you. Ask them what they would do and have a conversation to get them to come to their own conclusion?

It is likely that making an activity GREEN will take more time, in the short-term. Coaching someone to learn a new activity does tend to take longer. But if you improve a person, the likelihood of the interruption occurring again, due to them asking for your help, is significantly reduced. It's about investing time now to reap the rewards later.

Option two: Delegate it

> **ACTION:** Make sure the person you're delegating the activity to is informed and insert a MONITORING activity in your diary (if one doesn't already exist), at an appropriate point in time, to ensure that the new activity gets done.
>
> **COME BACK WHEN DONE.**

Option three: Don't do it at all

> **ACTION:** Make sure you're clear, with the person who interrupted you, that you're not taking on the new activity and explain why. Remember to do this considerately.
>
> **COME BACK WHEN DONE.**

You're Done!

That's it. If you use the Spot Diary Detox every time you get interrupted, or each time you have a conflict between two or more activities or appointments, you will stop to think about the impact on your time and ensure you make the best decision for you and your organisation.

SUMMARY

"Everywhere is within walking distance if you have the time."

Steven Wright

Your Diary Detox is complete, but the journey has really only just begun. You now have everything you need to get a day back in your diary every week. Your diary has been turned into a heat map that shows you if you're focusing your time on making your world better, keeping it the same, or making it worse.

You have the tools to:

- Fully understand what you need to do to achieve your targets

- Ensure that every activity you put in your diary has value and is aligned to achieving your targets

- Help you say no when you need to and minimise the impact of any interruption that comes your way.

Remember what the board director from the Introduction said, "It's simple, but not easy". Things are unlikely to be perfect straight away. Just remember to complete your Weekly Diary Detox every week. It's the one thing that will make sure you build your week on concrete foundations and will likely be the only time in your week where you get to focus on you and what you want to achieve. Once the Weekly Diary Detox becomes a regular habit in your week, everything else will start to fall into place.

You can delegate things that are best placed elsewhere. That delegation will empower your team to grow and contribute in ways they never have before. As a result, their engagement will go through the roof, as will their commitment to you and your organisation.

You will gain more time to help your team, and you'll be able to spend more time networking within and outside your organisation, perhaps for the first time ever. You'll be able to take the time to think about what is happening and what you should do next. You will also have the space to get involved and shape new initiatives within your organisation.

You can use the Diary Detox principles with your team as a structured way of having one-to-ones. Reviewing your team's diary activities using the Diary Detox Categories and colours will give you a way to discuss the value your team is adding. Extending the Diary Detox to your team gives them a way of holding themselves accountable every day too.

Once you have seen the value of your Diary Detox, you might decide to introduce it to others more senior in your organisation. You will be able to show the transformative impact it has had on your effectiveness at work. By trialling it with your peers, in situations similar to your own within the organisation, the Diary Detox will prove itself valuable and those peers might start to roll it out to all managers with a view to promoting a culture of improvement and leadership.

You'll have a choice over how much time you spend working and a choice over what you do with that time. It should feel incredibly liberating and empowering. Finally, you will be able to spend more time with your family and friends, enjoying life and each other.

Staying in touch

The best way to stay in touch is via social media. You can follow my personal journey, see videos and tips on the Diary Detox Categories – including strategies on what to do when things go wrong.

You'll also get early sight of developments with the Diary Detox including LIVING, the new BLUE Diary Detox Category, created to help with wellbeing and flexible working.

Please follow, share and engage

Facebook:	www.facebook.com/diarydetox
Instagram:	www.instagram.com/diary_detox/
Twitter:	www.twitter.com/diary_detox
LinkedIn:	www.linkedin.com/company/diarydetox
YouTube:	www.youTube.com/DiaryDetox
FAQs	www.DiaryDetox.com/FAQ

It's important that I understand how your Diary Detox journey is progressing. What's working and what could work better. This is part of my MONITORING. So, as they occur to you, please post any thoughts and feedback to the Diary Detox Twitter feed (@diary_detox).

Thanks for trusting me with your time.

Good luck and have fun!

APPENDICES

"Never memorise something that you can look up."

Albert Einstein

Appendix A – Diary Detox Categories

Floating
You're not adding value or you're
not sure what value you added

Thinking
You're taking time to think
about vision, strategy, a plan
or obstacles to achieving them

Communicating
You're meeting new people
or sharing new ideas within
or outside your organisation

Improving
You're learning, teaching, or
enhancing your organisation, what
it does or who it does it with

Monitoring
You're checking to see that
things are as expected

Directing
You're giving instruction or
assigning tasks

Doing
You're producing something or
carrying out a task

NOTE: To see colour versions of the following, visit www.DiaryDetox.com/resources/book.

Appendix B - Diary Detox Role Ratios

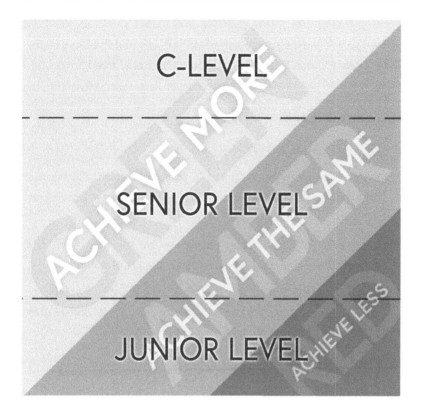

NOTE: To see colour versions of the following, visit www.DiaryDetox.com/resources/book.

89

Appendix C - Adding the Diary Detox Categories to your diary

Below you will find instructions that will help you add the Diary Detox Categories to your chosen diary. You should only need to do this once.

Microsoft Outlook

1. Open your Microsoft Outlook Calendar.

2. Right click on any appointment in your diary, select 'Categorise' and then select 'Edit Categories'. This should open a 'Categories' window.

3. Remove all of the existing categories by selecting each and clicking the '-' symbol at the bottom of the list of categories.

4. Click the '+' symbol at the bottom of the list of categories to add a new category. Add a new category using the same neutral colour (e.g. grey) for each of:
    *   THINKING
    *   COMMUNICATING
    *   IMPROVING
    *   MONITORING
    *   DIRECTING
    *   DOING
    *   FLOATING

    You should now have seven new categories, each having the same neutral colour. You will change the colours later.

5. Close the Categories window.

Apple iCloud

Within iCloud Calendar, adding each of the categories is done using multiple calendars as follows:

1. Open iCloud Calendar

2. Click 'Edit' in the left-hand bar.

3. Click the '+' symbol in the left-hand bar to add a new calendar.

4. Name the calendar using one of:
    *   THINKING
    *   COMMUNICATING
    *   IMPROVING
    *   MONITORING
    *   DIRECTING
    *   DOING
    *   FLOATING

5. Change the colour of the new calendar to blue.

6. Repeat for each category name.

You should now have seven new categories, each having the same blue colour.

Google Calendar

Within Google Calendar, adding each of the categories is done using multiple calendars as follows:

1. Open Google Calendar

2. Click the '+' symbol next to 'Other Calendars' in the left-hand bar to add a new calendar.

3. Click 'Create a new calendar'.

4. Name the calendar using one of:
   - THINKING
   - COMMUNICATING
   - IMPROVING
   - MONITORING
   - DIRECTING
   - DOING
   - FLOATING

5. Click 'Create Calendar'.

6. Repeat for each category name.

7. You should now have seven new categories. Click the left-hand arrow next to 'Settings' in the top left corner to return to the main calendar screen.

8. Hover your mouse-pointer over each of the new calendars in turn and click the three dots that you see appear.

9. Change the colour to blue.

You should now have seven new categories, each having the same blue colour.

Appendix D - Adding the colours to your Diary Detox Categories

Below you will find instructions that will help you add the correct colour to your Diary Detox Categories in your chosen diary.

Microsoft Outlook

1. Open your Microsoft Outlook Calendar

2. Right click on any appointment in your diary, select 'Categorise' and then select 'Edit Categories'. This should open a 'Categories' window.

3. Select the colour next to each Diary Detox category and set as follows:
    - THINKING (Green)
    - COMMUNICATING (Green)
    - IMPROVING (Green)
    - MONITORING (Amber)
    - DIRECTING (Amber)
    - DOING (Red)
    - FLOATING (Brown)

4. Close the Categories window (the colours will not appear in your diary until you complete this step).

Apple iCloud

1. Open iCloud Calendar

2. Click 'Edit' in the left-hand bar.

3. Click the coloured dot symbol in the left-hand bar next to each calendar and set as follows:
    - THINKING (Green)
    - COMMUNICATING (Green)
    - IMPROVING (Green)

- MONITORING (Amber)
- DIRECTING (Amber)
- DOING (Red)
- FLOATING (Brown)

4. Click 'Done' in the left-hand bar.

Google Calendar

1. Open Google Calendar

2. Hover your mouse-pointer over each of the new calendars in turn and click the three dots that you see appear.

3. Set the colour as follows:
   - THINKING (Green)
   - COMMUNICATING (Green)
   - IMPROVING (Green)
   - MONITORING (Amber)
   - DIRECTING (Amber)
   - DOING (Red)
   - FLOATING (Brown)

Appendix E - Your Weekly Diary Detox Checklist

Diary	Ensure everything you did **this** week is in your diary Ensure **next** week's commitments are in your diary	☐ ☐
Evaluate	Ensure this week's categories are still correct Categorise all of next week's activities	☐ ☐
Target	Review your Targets and change if necessary Erase the ticks from the 'In Diary' column	☐ ☐
Opportunity	Tick or cross 'In Diary' for each target depending on whether present in **next** week's Diary	☐
X-change	In 1, 2, 3 order, insert and activity in your diary for each target with a cross and **tick when inserted** Reflect on your colour mix against Roles Ratios Fill remaining space with 'green' activities	☐ ☐ ☐

Appendix F - Commonly used information

Your desired working hours

Day	Start Time	Finish Time
Monday		
Tuesday		
Wednesday		
Thursday		
Friday		
Saturday		
Sunday		

Your desired Diary Detox Colour Mix

Colour	Percentage or Days (per week)
GREEN (LEADING)	
AMBER (MANAGING)	
RED (DOING)	

488469

Your Diary Detox Targets

Who?	Target	In Diary?
Tanya		
Nikki	Roles halved	
	Changed processes without PM	

Who will do it?

For someone else to do → I will do because there's no one else → That's for me, and only me

ACKNOWLEDGEMENTS

Without my wife, Emma, this book would not exist. Two years ago, she offered to take up the slack while I took the leap and left my 20-year career to start my own business. Without her faith and incredible support, I would never have found the Diary Detox.

My family and friends have also been so important to this journey. There are too many of you to mention individually, but you each know who you are and what you mean to me.

In the early days, I struggled to find a way to tell the world about Diary Detox. Then, I met Rachel Savage. She showed me the power of the 'Hero's Journey' and convinced me that you, the reader, are the hero of your story, not me. In our first session Rachel said, "You know there's a book in this don't you?". I do now.

Writing down my thoughts was one thing but having the confidence to share them with the world is another. Without Gabriella Hadley, my editor, who voluntarily gave many hours to help me, I don't know when, or if, I would have been ready. Gabriella's incredible generosity, patience and expertise are, and will remain, so very much appreciated.

Lastly, to everyone who said they were too busy to meet me when I first started my business. It's because of you all that the seed of an idea was planted that has now grown into the Diary Detox.

Thank you.

Paul Holbrook is a time rebel and leadership disrupter who, after 20 years in change management in the City of London, decided that he'd simply had enough of standing by, watching the toxic effects of people's diaries on themselves and those around them. From that moment, he decided he wanted to spend his time creating a world of better-led people.

Having covered a variety of roles within technology and people management, Paul is passionate about improvement. He believes the only thing stopping people getting the most from themselves, is an unerring attention to getting the best from everyone and everything around them. It all starts with what's in their own diary.

Paul is an all-round optimist and the creator of the Diary Detox®.